The World of Dinosaurs

Richard Moody B.Sc., Ph.D.
illustrated by Victor Ambrus

diagrams drawn by Bob Mathias

Hamlyn
London · New York · Sydney · Toronto

Contents

Introduction 4
Men and the Dinosaurs 5
Towards the Dinosaurs 9
The Family of Reptiles 13
Dawn of the Terrible Lizards 16
Dinosaurs Rule the Earth 21
A Period of Change 29
The Dinosaurs Vanish. We Ask Why? 40
The Age of Mammals 44
Index 46

Introduction

The story of the dinosaurs is part of the history of life on our Earth. This history or record started with very simple animals or plants and continues today with man and the various other animals and plants that live around us. Dinosaurs are found as fossils in many parts of the world, sometimes as single bones, or more rarely as complete skeletons with skin. From these specimens scientists can tell the size and shape of the animal and the way it fed and walked. But because the dinosaurs have vanished from the face of the Earth, much of the information on how and where they lived is lost. Therefore, some of the ideas put forward in this book are only possible answers to what actually happened. They are, however, based on evidence found in rocks.

The story of the dinosaurs is forever changing as more and more fossils are discovered and the knowledge of scientists increases. Perhaps one day you will discover many important things about these incredible reptiles.

Men and the Dinosaurs

The title of this chapter suggests that men and the dinosaurs lived at the same time. But as the last dinosaur lived over 60 million years ago, it would be wrong to think that this was true, especially as man is a relatively new animal on the planet Earth. The title refers to the fantastic tales of discoveries that have taken place since man found the first dinosaur bone.

We think of the dinosaurs as fearsome, ferocious animals of enormous size and with violent habits. These thoughts are due to a mixture of folklore and fantasy. In fact, the truth is that huge, vicious dinosaurs did roam the Earth, but they did so in the company of small bird-like relatives. Some dinosaurs ate meat, hunted and killed their prey, but others were peaceful animals, eating plants and basking in the hot sun.

Above William Buckland (1784–1856)

Below Gideon Mantell (1790–1852)

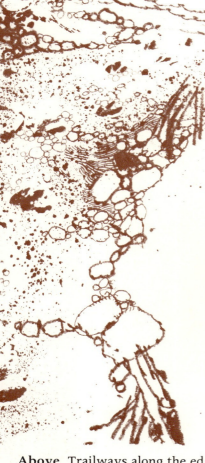

Above Trailways along the edge of a Jurassic lake. Traces such as these have been found in Dorset and in Connecticut, U.S.A. They were probably made by *Megalosaurus*.

The story of the dinosaurs is quite a recent one; it is based on the discoveries of bones and skeletons throughout the world. At first the finds were rare and the story confused, but gradually new and more valuable discoveries revealed a story of untold interest.

The first bone was found in 1676, just three hundred years ago. It was a piece of leg bone and for a long time after its discovery in the county of Oxfordshire, England, it was thought to be part of a giant man.

Other finds were also wrongly identified and some three-toed footprints found in America were thought to belong to 'Noah's Raven', an obvious reference to the Ark and its captain.

As time progressed, knowledge increased and men like William Buckland and Gideon Mantell made very important discoveries in England before 1830. Both men were enthusiastic palaeontologists (pay–lee–on–tol–o–gists), people who study fossils. William Buckland was also a dean and Gideon Mantell a doctor of medicine. The bones found by Buckland were named *Megalosaurus* (Meg–al–o–saw–rus) because the name suggests that the animal was very large (Megalo = big, sauros = lizard).

Above The Maidstone coat of arms with *Iguanodon* as the left support.
(*Coat of arms reproduced by courtesy of Maidstone Borough Council.*)

Below Dinosaur models were built by Waterhouse Hawkins and exhibited in the grounds of Sydenham Park, London.

Dr Mantell's interest in fossils increased when his wife discovered teeth of a giant reptile while out walking near Cuckfield in Sussex. He identified the teeth and named the animal to which they belonged *Iguanodon* (Ig–u–are–no–don), a giant Cretaceous plant-eater which we will meet again during our story. Dr Mantell chose the name *Iguanodon* because the teeth found by his wife were very much like the teeth of the living iguana lizard.

Imagine the excitement of finding the first bones of such a giant reptile. It was the start of a great detective story.

More clues to *Iguanodon* were found near Maidstone, Kent, in 1834. Then, the town was a coach journey from London. The roads were rough and often needed repair and rock for filling potholes came from local quarries.

One day, after blasting, the bones of a giant animal were found and collected by a local man, Mr Binstead, and carefully moved to a safe place. Sometime later Mr Binstead wrote a letter to Mantell describing his discovery and Mantell, eager to obtain the specimens, journeyed to Maidstone. After offers of £10 and £20, Binstead accepted £25, which was a great deal of money in those days. The specimens were removed to Brighton, where Dr Mantell spent several months preparing the bones with a hammer and chisel, lifting small chips of rock with each blow.

This story tells us two things. The first is that fossil hunters are dedicated people; the second, that in the past the collection and preparation of specimens was very difficult.

To mark the discovery of the dinosaur bones, Maidstone has included *Iguanodon* in its coat of arms.

Other giant reptile bones were found between 1830 and 1840. These were studied by a very famous palaeontologist, Sir Richard Owen. Sir Richard claimed they belonged to a group of extinct fossil reptiles which he named the Dinosauria. This name means 'terrible lizards', although scientists now know that the dinosaurs were not lizards, but a separate and distinct group of reptiles.

Think of the shock Londoners experienced in 1854 when Owen exhibited models of the gigantic reptiles at Crystal Palace. A fantastic relationship with the public had begun.

These models are still on view at Crystal Palace, but many, more accurate models are to be seen in resorts throughout the world.

Dinosaur discoveries continued throughout the last century. Many new types of 'terrible lizards' were uncovered, some even more spectacular than those known before. We shall see them later.

In America during the 1870s and 1880s great finds were made by Professors Marsh and Cope. These discoveries took place in the west of that great continent. Marsh and Cope competed against each other, each trying to find bigger and better specimens. It is said that their workmen fought with their fists against each other.

For men like Marsh and Cope their rivalry acted as a spur to achieve greater things. At the time when they searched for the bones of dinosaurs, Sittingbull and his Sioux Indians were fighting Custer. Incredibly, Cope looked for and found many of his specimens in Indian country, with the warring tribes camped only a few miles from his dig. He did receive some protection, however, from the United States 7th Cavalry.

The Americans found many fossil graveyards. The most impressive is now known as the Dinosaur National Monument, in Utah, U.S.A. The Museum built there covers a mountain of bones of animals that lived 150 million years ago.

The first major find made there was in the summer of 1909; it was a dinosaur's tail discovered by the famous geologist Earl Douglass. Dr Douglass spent some very cold winters digging away at this incredible mountain of bones. His wife and small baby lived with him in a tent.

The finds from Utah filled museums. Three hundred tonnes alone went to the Carnegie Museum in Pittsburgh, U.S.A.

From other discoveries in Europe and America more and more information on the dinosaurs came to light. In certain cases this information was of value in understanding the way some dinosaurs lived, in others it added greatly to the knowledge of body shapes and structure. Two discoveries, one in Belgium, the other in North America, illustrate these points.

Top Othniel Charles Marsh (1831–1899)

Above Edward Drinker Cope (1840–1897)

Below Men still work on the great piles of bones found near Vernal, Utah by Earl Douglass.

The Belgian find took place in 1878 when coal miners were making a mine shaft larger. Deep below the surface, in a narrow tunnel, they came across a collection of large bones. They told the mine managers, who in turn informed the Natural History Museum in Brussels. The bones were identified as *Iguanodon*, the same type of animal as that found at Maidstone. The bones in the Belgian mine shaft belonged to more than one individual and further digging showed that the miners had discovered something remarkable, which was to provide a great deal of information on the area where the animals lived and on the way they walked and the food they ate. A second, lower tunnel at 356 metres led the museum collectors to more bones. Obviously, the find was a fossil graveyard.

These animals were buried in rocks younger in age than those normally dug by the miners. From the way the younger rocks filled a wedge-shaped feature in the coal, it was possible to reconstruct the landscape at the time the iguanodonts lived. Across this landscape a large ravine occurred, into which a number of animals had slipped or fallen, had died and were buried in the layers of mud which filled the deep chasm. The animals were found in the position of death, but their bones were close together as they would have been in life. These specimens were removed to the museum in Brussels.

Today, eleven iguanodonts stand tall in the Natural History Museum in Brussels, and another twenty specimens, discovered over 300 metres below ground level, near the town of Bernissart, are exhibited in the position in which they were found.

The North American discovery took place thirty years later in southern Wyoming. Unlike the Belgian discovery, only one animal was found, but it was just as important because it provided paleontologists with the first mummified dinosaur. The fossil was found by George and Levi Sternberg in 1908 and consisted of the skeleton of a duckbilled dinosaur 'wrapped' in skin. The Sternbergs were overjoyed by their discovery and it was a just reward for months of very hard work. Like other workers, they camped in the wild and often had to put up with a meagre diet.

The Sternberg specimen is now housed in the American Museum of Natural History in New York. Many other museums throughout the world, however, have specimens collected by the Sternberg family.

Dinosaur bones have now been found in many lands and collecting continues. Instead of using only hammers and chisels finds are now prepared with drills, mechanical pencils, and powders blasted onto the surrounding sediment at high pressure. Dilute acids are also used which eat away at the sediments surrounding the bones. Bones prepared in acid look like the skeletons of animals that died yesterday. The information paleontologists receive from these beautiful specimens is very helpful in reconstructing the animal.

New discoveries continue the story of where and how the dinosaurs lived. The relationship between men and the dinosaurs is one of awe.

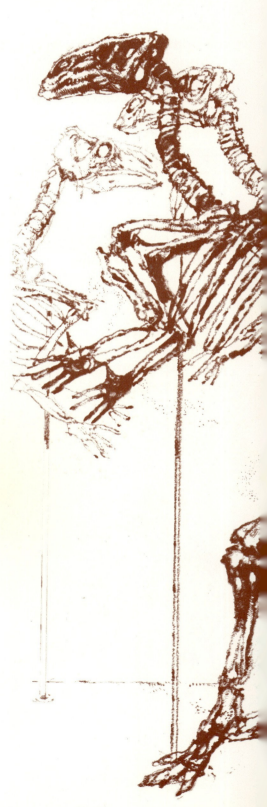

Below Skeletons of *Iguanodon* as displayed at the Natural History Museum, Brussels.

Towards the Dinosaurs

When man could draw and paint, he drew pictures of his everyday life. He also made beautiful paintings of the animals that lived around him and some of these are preserved on the walls of caves; examples have been found near Altamira, Spain, and Lascaux, France. Our cave artist was the first historian. Before him the incredible story of bygone ages was preserved only in rocks, known as sediments, deposited on the surface of the Earth's crust. When animals and plants die, they may be buried in sediments, the layers of which build up like pages in a book. The animals and plants become fossils. They are the words of geological history.

Right The sequence of events that take place after the death of an animal which may lead to it being preserved as a fossil. It is essential that burial is rapid and the carcass be protected from the weather and scavengers.

The age of the Earth is thought to be 4,500 million years. But life began much later, about 2,500 million years ago. Earth scientists and palaeontologists believe that the first form of life was the result of a long period of chemical evolution. The chemicals occurred naturally in the atmosphere of the young planet and, with the help of rain, accumulated in the seas. Time and selection resulted in the development of simple plants and animals, and once these lowly living things had developed the succession of life was under way. In a time of environmental change animals with certain characters survive whilst others fail and die out. Over many generations these characters may change slightly and a new form of animal may be created. This is a simple explanation of the process of evolution.

Below The animals and plants on our time chart indicate the variety of fossils found in the sediments of past ages.

The chart on this page shows the history of life. It also divides geological time into the main periods and eras. To illustrate the life of one man on the chart is impossible; geologically it lasts only one second.

Eras	Invertebrate and Plant Life	Vertebrate Life
Cainozoic/Quaternary Pleistocene present day to 2 million years ago	*Pupilla* (gastropod), *Balanophyllia* (coral)	Mackerel, Sabre-tooth tiger, Woolly mammoth, *Australopithecus*
Cainozoic/Tertiary Pliocene 2–7 million years ago	*Arctica* (bivalve), *Balanus* (barnacle)	Giraffe, *Alticamelus* (camel), *Pliohippus* (horse)
Miocene 7–26 million years ago	Oak leaf, Crab, *Terebratula* (brachiopod)	*Latimeria* (fish), *Merychippus* (horse), *Moropus* (rhinoceros)
Oligocene 26–38 million years ago	*Pecten* (bivalve), *Cornulina* (gastropod)	*Phenacodus* (mammal), *Archaeotherium* (pig?)
Eocene and Palaeocene 38–65 million years ago	*Aralia* (plant), Hexacoral	*Eohippus* (horse), *Diatryma* (bird), *Puppigerus* (turtle)
Mesozoic Cretaceous 65–136 million years ago	*Micraster* (echinoid), *Hamites* (ammonite)	*Triceratops* (dinosaur), *Pteranodon* (reptile), *Iguanodon* (dinosaur)
Jurassic 136–193 million years ago	*Gryphaea* (bivalve), *Dactylioceras* (ammonite)	*Apatosaurus* (dinosaur), *Stegosaurus* (dinosaur), *Allosaurus* (dinosaur)
Triassic 193–225 million years ago	*Ceratites* (ammonite), *Chlamys* (bivalve)	*Rutiodon* (phytosaur), *Cynognathus* (reptile), *Ornithosuchus* (reptile)
Palaeozoic/Upper Permian 225–280 million years ago	*Horridonia* (brachiopod)	*Elginia* (reptile), *Dimetrodon* (reptile), *Endothiodon* (reptile)
Carboniferous 280–345 million years ago	*Productus* (brachiopod), *Lithostrotion* (coral), *Lepidodendron* (tree)	*Cornuboniscus* (fish), *Eumicrerpeton* (amphibian)
Devonian 345–395 million years ago	*Phacops* (trilobite), *Favosites* (coral), *Manticoceras* (goniatite)	*Hemicyclaspis* (fish), *Holoptychius* (fish)
Palaeozoic/Lower Silurian 395–435 million years ago	*Monograptus* (graptolite), *Halysites* (coral)	*Pteraspis* (fish), *Jaymotius* (fish)
Ordovician 435–500 million years ago	*Onnia* (trilobite), *Didymograptus* (graptolite)	
Cambrian 500–570 million years ago	*Olenellus* (trilobite), *Lingulella* (brachiopod)	
Pre-Cambrian 570–4600 (?) million years ago	Worms	

Apart from a few discoveries of soft-bodied animals, such as jelly-fish, the imprints of which are recorded in Pre-Cambrian rocks, it is not until animals and plants deposited skeletons, formed of different mineral substances, that the number of fossils really increased. These skeletons were used for protection and support. This happened some 570 million years ago at the start of the Cambrian Period. Cambrian animals had no back-bones, their skeletons were deposited around the soft tissues. Trilobites and algal balls are fossil examples of Cambrian animals and plants.

During the millions of years that have passed between the Cambrian and now, many changes in the shapes of animals have occurred. Scientists can spot these changes and after identifying the fossil can use it, wherever it is found, to tell the age of the rocks in which it is discovered.

Animals with bony skeletons did not appear until well into the Ordovician Period, some 100 million years after the start of the Cambrian. The first records are very poor. Only small scales and single bones of 'fish' tell of the start of vertebrate history. It is unknown whether the first fish lived in the seas or in fresh water.

The story of fossil fish improves in the Devonian Period, when the number and variety of forms increases dramatically, perhaps due to the lack of direct competitors. The most primitive fish were the ostracoderms (os–tra–co–derms). They had heavy armour over much of their bodies and, unlike man or the reptiles, they had no jaws. The sucker-like mouth was on the underside of the head. For fish, they were poor swimmers.

Later, more agile fish with jaws appeared in the seas of the world. *Dinichthys* (Din–ick–this), a 'plated skin' fish, was typical of these new forms. It grew to a length of 10 metres. Amongst the other new forms were the first sharks and the bony fish.

Some fish with bony skeletons have ray-like fins; in others the fins are lobe-like. Some bony fish developed lungs.

Lungfish, similar to *Dipterus* (Dip–ter–rus) of the Middle Devonian, live today in South America, Africa and Australia. In times when the water in which they live dries up, they can survive in burrows. In their burrows they are protected against enemies and against the hard climatic conditions.

Latimeria (La–tim–e–ree–a) is an example of a lobe-finned fish. This 'living fossil' was first discovered in 1938 off the coast of South Africa and is very much like its fossil relatives. The lobe-fins are an important step in the development of legs.

The appearance of lungs and the development of legs show that some fish were changing into the first amphibians. This change was probably encouraged by the climate of the Devonian Period. Ponds and streams would often dry up at this time and to survive animals would have to drag themselves across the land to a new pool. The early amphibians, such as *Ichthyostega* (Ick–thee–o–ste–ga), had well developed limbs to help them in their movements, but were restricted in that they still had to lay their fish-like eggs in water.

Ichthyostega

Latimeria

Dipterus

Dinichthys

Pteraspis
an example of a jawless fish

Algal ball

Trilobite

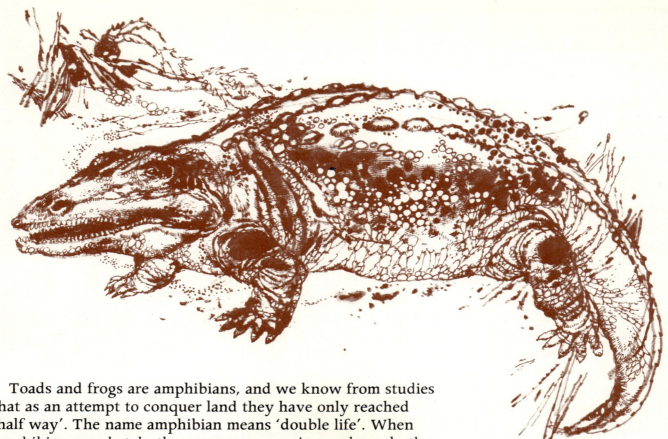

Above *Eryops* – a Permian amphibian

Toads and frogs are amphibians, and we know from studies that as an attempt to conquer land they have only reached 'half way'. The name amphibian means 'double life'. When amphibian eggs hatch, the young grow up in ponds; only the adult is able to live on land.

During the Palaeozoic Era (the time of ancient life), which extended from the Cambrian to the end of the Permian Period, plants as well as animals spread onto the land. The first plants were small, with small leaves, the whole plant being protected against the rays of the sun by a thick outer cover.

In the Carboniferous, fern-like plants grew to enormous sizes and vast areas of the Earth's surface were covered in swampy forests. The Carboniferous is also called the Coal Age, for it was then that the majority of plant material that forms the coal beds of many regions of the world was deposited.

The warm, humid conditions that existed in the Carboniferous were ideal for the amphibians, which needed to keep their skins moist, and many new forms arose. Some of them were small like the frogs; some, like *Eryops* (Er–ee–ops) in the Permian, grew to 3 metres in length.

To live on land successfully, animals needed to protect their eggs against drying out. Some amphibians must have succeeded in this, protecting their eggs with a shell case. The young animals developed inside the shell. They had their own food supply and were able to breathe through the shell. These animals could live all of their lives on land; they could go where they pleased. Some fed on plants, others on the insects which now swarmed in the new forests; some ate each other. These animals were the earliest reptiles. Unlike the amphibians they developed scaly skins and breathed through lungs throughout their life history.

Proof that reptiles lay eggs is seen today when turtles drag themselves up onto beaches of the Atlantic and Pacific Oceans to lay their eggs in the sand.

Below The green turtle lays eggs in the sands of an Atlantic beach.

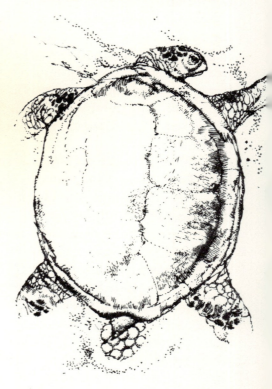

The Family of Reptiles

If one imagines the number of animals that exist today and the different lives they lead, it is not difficult to believe that if animals like the reptiles had no real competitors, they could soon change and fill all of the new places available to them. 300 million years ago the lands lay open to the reptiles and they evolved in many different ways to take advantage of the new habitats that lay before them.

Think of the things they ate. Through a number of links it is possible to construct a chain of feeding habits. These chains, or perhaps webs would be a better term, have existed throughout time.

Animals that eat plants are called herbivores. Some fossil reptiles are known to have eaten plants, and as a result they were often very big, with large bellies to digest the vast amounts of food they ate.

Animals that eat meat are called carnivores; they are often hunters. To live, they must trap and kill their food. Many reptiles preserved in the fossil record were carnivores. To catch their prey they had to move quickly. They also developed sharp teeth for biting, tearing and ripping.

Reptiles had solved the problems of living on land and so had plants. Forests had spread far and wide and the plant-eating reptiles were certain of abundant food. In turn, they were on the menu of the flesh eaters.

The chart on this page plots the evolution of the different groups of reptiles. At first, many reptiles were slow-moving animals, with large heavy bones. They are called cotylosaurs (co–tile–o–saws) or 'stem reptiles' (those from which many branches originated). Their shoulder bones and limbs acted like girders lifting the heavy body off the ground.

Cotylosaurs like *Pareiasaurus* (Par–rye–a–saw–rus) lived

Above *Pareiasaurus* – Upper Permian

Below The family tree of the reptiles.

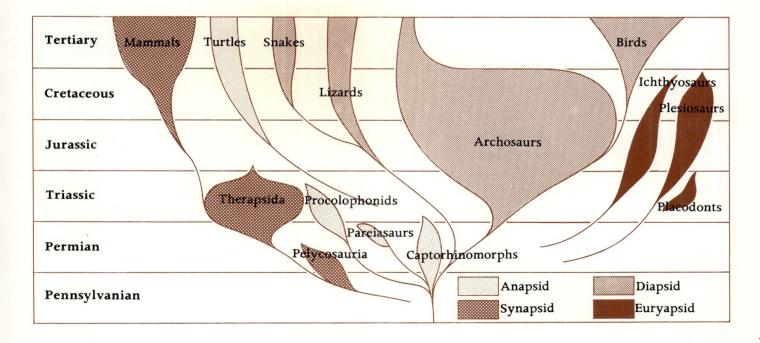

in hot, dry areas. Their bones have been discovered in America and South Africa in rocks of Permian age.

From these 'stem reptiles' many different types arose. Some were four legged, whilst others ran on two legs. Some returned to the sea and lived like the dolphins, seals and whales of today. One group, the synapsids (si–nap–sids), were to change step by step to become mammals. These can be considered as the first rung on the ladder to man.

Turtles, snakes and lizards arose directly from the cotylosaurs, but crocodiles and pterosaurs (ter–ro–saws) have the same ancestors as the dinosaurs. These are called the thecodonts (thee–co–donts) which themselves developed from the 'stem reptiles'. We shall describe the thecodonts later.

The seas of the late Palaeozoic and early Mesozoic Eras were like larders full of fish. Some reptiles returned to the seas, first to feed and then to live. The first were hunter-killers. They were followed by types that ate plants and shell-fish.

To be able to crush shells, these animals needed strong jaws and teeth. One group, the placodonts (plak–o–donts), developed large flat teeth. They broke the shells from the rocks with their strong beaks and crushed them in their mouths. Some placodonts look very much like turtles.

With so many types of reptiles to be found in the fossil record, it is necessary to place them into families. This is done by finding out all the important characters of the different animals and using them to link one form with another. Palaeontologists can divide the reptiles into major groups on the characters of the skull.

Four kinds of skulls are recognised in reptiles, and the drawing on this page shows that it is easy to spot the differences, for example, between the skulls of turtles and dinosaurs.

Also each modification in the overall skeleton of a reptile will help in classification, as it could mean a change of shape and a significant difference between a reptile and its nearest relative.

Changes and differences in the skeleton are also used to place the dinosaurs into different families, and in turn into one of two major orders, depending on the nature of their hip bones. One of these major orders is called the Ornithischia (Or–nith–ish–ee–are) or 'bird-hipped' dinosaurs, whilst the other is known as the Saurischia (Saw–rish–ee–are) or 'lizard-hipped'.

To understand the development of these two types of hip, one must first know something of the ancestors of the dinosaurs. They were called the thecodonts, or 'teeth in sockets' reptiles. Their limbs were strong and enabled the animals to run quickly; their hip bones were somewhat lizard-like. Most of these reptiles had much lighter skeletons than those of the 'stem reptiles', and a few began to run on two legs. At first, this was for short distances only but as time progressed this posture was adopted permanently.

To be able to run properly on its hind legs, the animal's limbs would have to be underneath the body. This would involve changes in the muscle pattern and the shape of the hip bones. Both two- and four-legged animals are included in a group called the pseudosuchian (sue–do–sue–key–an) thecodonts

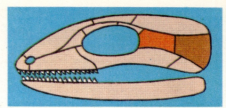
Anapsid skull as found in turtles

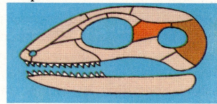
Synapsid skull as found in mammal-like reptiles

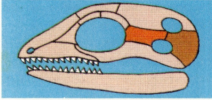
Diapsid skull as found in dinosaurs

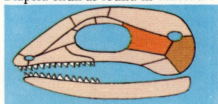
Euryapsid skull as found in plesiosaurs

Above The four basic types of skull found in living and fossil reptiles. In each type the bone pattern differs behind the eye.

Saltoposuchus an example of a pseudosuchian thecodont

and it is probable that both dinosaur orders evolved from this group. The two hip types indicate an early division within the ancestors of the dinosaurs, with one branch, the ornithischians, showing a radical change in their hip structure. Because of this radical change the ornithischians could be regarded as specialised and the saurischians as being closer to early ancestral forms.

Many early 'bird-hipped' dinosaurs were two-legged, but during their history a number of species returned to a four-legged posture. Within the 'lizard-hipped' Saurischia both two and four-legged dinosaurs were known also. This information is based on the differences in the skeletons, the story of the reptile family being based on the recording of such differences. To know where each animal or its brothers and sisters lived, accurate recognition is essential. The search for the clues is an exciting one and takes place in many parts of the world.

With this knowledge we have of the family of reptiles and the history of our planet, we can now take a much closer look at the times when the dinosaurs roamed on Earth.

Below This illustration shows us how the two dinosaur groups, the Saurischia and the Ornithischia, developed from a common ancestral stock. We can also see the differences between the hip-bones of the two types and that both two and four-legged animals are known from each group.

Ornithischia
Thecodontia
Saurischia

Stegosaurus
an example of a quadrupedal ornithischian

Corythosaurus
an example of an ornithischian ornithopod

Apatosaurus
an example of a saurischian sauropod

Tyrannosaurus
an example of a saurischian theropod

Dawn of the Terrible Lizards

The Triassic Period, 193–225 million years ago

Below The dots on the map show the areas where the Triassic dinosaurs lived.

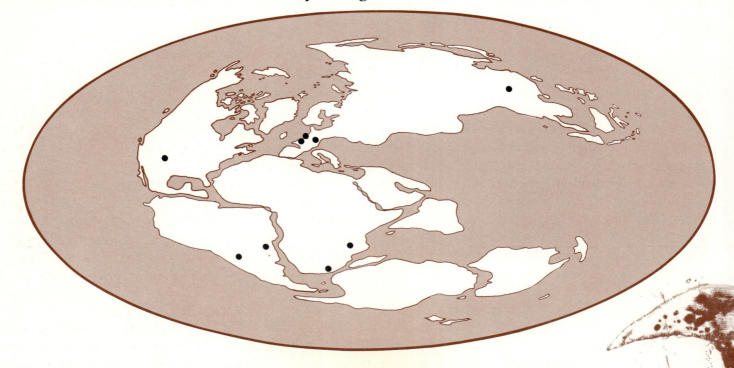

Ichthyosaur

From evidence collected in the study of rocks from the Triassic Period, we can reconstruct a story which took place many millions of years ago. The map of the world on this page shows that the continents were not in the same positions as today.

Many of the lands in the Triassic were like deserts, with few plants and lots of sand. Now and then heavy rains would fall, causing flooding and the formation of temporary lakes and salt-water pools. Oases were also present, together with coal-forming swamps. The land masses were surrounded by seas in which a variety of plants and animals lived.

Clues to the hot, dry climate of those far-off days include the red colour of the rocks, and salt which was deposited in many regions. Rain pits and fossil footprints are also known, indicating that after flooding, droughts occurred; mud cracks support this evidence.

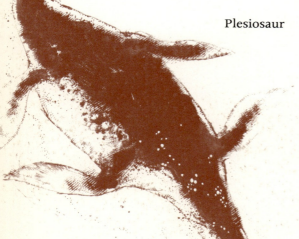

Plesiosaur

The fossil footprints or 'trace fossils' show that new types of animals made their first appearance at this time. Bones and shells confirm the presence of these and other new forms.

Amongst these are the ichthyosaurs (ick–thee–o–saws) and plesiosaurs (please–ee–o–saws), and the ancestors of the crocodiles, pterosaurs, and dinosaurs. The reptiles were the dominant group and the Triassic is the start of the 'Age of Reptiles', which lasted for over 150 million years and apart from the Triassic, included the Jurassic and Cretaceous Periods.

We know reptiles began before the Triassic, and therefore it is important to question how and why the early relatives of the dinosaurs took the place of other successful groups.

We have seen that early reptiles were often heavily built with their limbs placed well away from the body. They walked like modern newts and salamanders. The ancestors of the dinosaurs, the thecodonts, improved on this by bringing their limbs closer to the body. This helped them to move more quickly and to catch and eat slower animals.

The thecodonts were meat-eaters, and, unlike earlier reptiles, their teeth were set in deep sockets. Throughout their lives, these teeth were replaced by new ones from below. A simple experiment with a small tube and two pencils will serve to explain this process. Take a pencil, and place it in a tube which is slightly shorter in length. Then push the second pencil into the tube from below. The original pencil, like the old tooth, is pushed out and the new one takes its place.

The thecodonts were more advanced reptiles; their new limb structure, the deep-set teeth and armoured skin helped them to become truly successful. A typical thecodont was *Mandasuchus* (Man–da–sue–kus), which grew to the size of a crocodile. It lived over 200 million years ago, but unlike the crocodile it lived most of its life on land. *Mandasuchus* was a member of the pseudosuchian thecodonts, the group from which both the crocodiles and dinosaurs developed.

Other pseudosuchians were *Ornithosuchus* (Or–nith–o–sue–kus) and *Staganolepis* (Stag–an–o–leep–is), and they show that different types of animal occur within the same group.

Ornithosuchus was lightly built and walked on two legs; in our picture it looks a very active little character. It is reasonable to assume that this animal could easily be the great-grandparent of the small meat-eating dinosaurs of later times. *Staganolepis*, on the other hand, was like *Mandasuchus* and walked on all fours; its back was armoured for protection.

The pseudosuchians lived in the same areas as another thecodont group called the phytosaurs (fie–toe–saws). At first sight these animals look very similar to the crocodiles, but differences do occur, for their nostrils are placed just in front of the eyes and their hind limbs are very long. A typical phytosaur is *Phytosaurus* (Fie–toe–saw–rus); its long limbs and high-placed nostrils were ideal for a life in water. The long snout, with rows of sharp teeth, would quickly dispose of any fish that swam too close.

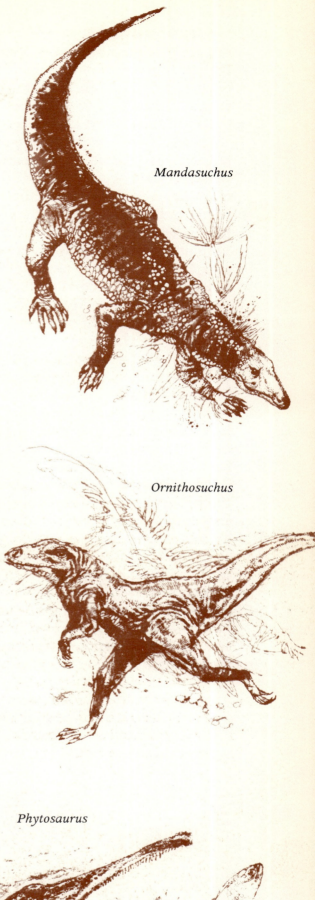

Mandasuchus

Ornithosuchus

Phytosaurus

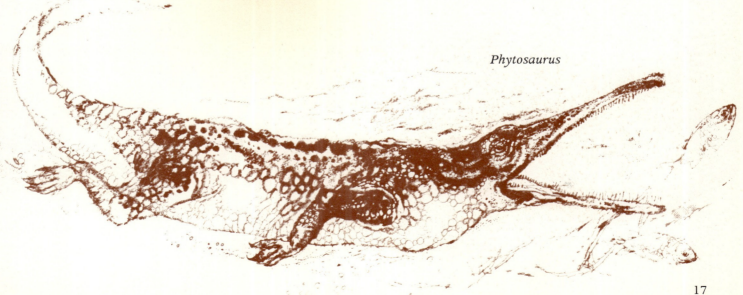

Like *Ornithosuchus* and *Mandasuchus*, *Phytosaurus* was replaced by more advanced animals by the end of the Triassic Period. In the case of the phytosaurs, the true crocodiles evolved to occupy their habitats, whilst the pseudosuchians found it impossible to compete with the early dinosaurs.

One of the earliest known dinosaurs is *Plateosaurus* (Plat–ee–o–saw–rus). It is very large in comparison with its distant relatives, with adult forms reaching 6 metres in length. In the Upper Triassic we would have found *Plateosaurus* at the side of a lake, feeding on soft plants, such as ferns, cycads (tree ferns) and horsetails. It uses its long neck to reach a clump of plants; the head is small and the peg-like teeth crush the soft vegetation. When feeding and moving around within a small area the animal walks on all four legs. Sometimes, however, it stands or moves around on the back legs only. *Plateosaurus* is very much like the gigantic sauropods of later times.

Meat-eaters would sometimes force *Plateosaurus* to seek refuge in the waters of the lake. There, its bulky form would be quite safe from the more active land-dwelling carnivores. The latter are small for dinosaurs, the adults being around 3 metres in length. *Coelophysis* (Seal–o–fie–sis) is such an animal. It ran about on two legs, the arms were short and the hands could probably grip lumps of meat. As it eats, the teeth appear to saw through the flesh, each tooth being edged with fine saw-like projections.

The appearance of *Plateosaurus* and *Coelophysis* heralds the start of the long saurischian history. Both 'lizard-hipped' and 'bird-hipped' dinosaurs had appeared by the end of the Triassic Period.

The first ornithischians were plant-eaters and they lived at the same time as *Plateosaurus*, some 200 million years ago. At first, they were quite small, measuring about 2 metres from the nose to the tip of the tail. *Heterodontosaurus* (Het–er–ro–dont–o–saw–rus) and *Fabrosaurus* (Fab–row–saw–rus) illustrate that two basic types roamed the lands of the southern continents.

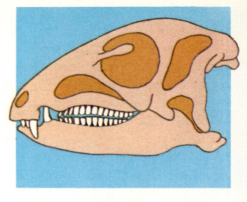

Above The skull of *Heterodontosaurus* showing the sabre-like teeth.

Below Beside a Triassic lake two large plateosaurids feed on the lush vegetation; a small carnivore, *Coelophysis*, hunts nearby and a phytosaur swims in the quiet waters.

The very name *Heterodontosaurus* suggests to the palaeontologists an animal with different types of teeth, and the illustration on page 18 shows this to be true. The jaws have long sabre-like teeth just in front of the more typical grinding types. The sabre-like teeth may suggest meat eating but it is much more likely that they were used as digging tools. The modern pig feeds in a similar manner.

Fabrosaurus lacks the sabre-like dentition of its cousin; it simply cuts and grinds the soft vegetation between rows of flattened teeth.

The ornithischians and saurischians continue to increase in numbers and variety from this time onwards. They will rule the lands of the Jurassic and Cretaceous Periods. Their appearance in the Triassic heralds a long and successful reign, but it is really only one important rung in the long ladder of evolution.

The Triassic could be described as having many such 'rungs', for before the dinosaurs we saw that their ancestors, the thecodonts, had replaced the mammal-like reptiles as the most important group. Some of the mammal-like forms survived into the Jurassic, but in real terms their day had passed.

Below These tiny mammals are *Megazostrodon*; to scientists they are an important link in the chain of evolution.

The mammals, in the form of *Megazostrodon* (Meg–a–zoss–troe–don) and its cousins, evolved from these reptilian ancestors over 200 million years ago.

How strange it must have been to be a small furry mammal among monsters such as *Plateosaurus* and the phytosaurs. It is thought that *Megazostrodon* and others were shy, nocturnal creatures which fed on insects and plants. During the day they could have been attacked by the two-legged meat-eaters like *Coelophysis* and its relatives.

Other changes in the Triassic Period include the replacement of the phytosaurs by the crocodiles and the appearance of the first flying reptiles.

In the seas, reptiles became the dominant group. New forms such as the ichthyosaurs, plesiosaurs and turtles appeared in the oceans of the world. The ichthyosaurs or 'fish lizards' were very well adapted for life in the water, their bodies being beautifully streamlined. They were much more common than either of the other two groups at the end of the Triassic Period.

The changes in the fossil record that took place in the Triassic may have been due to a number of things. Some scientists believe that the dry, arid conditions led to increased competition for food and eventual dominance by the most capable animals. The success of the dinosaurs was possibly due to the type of heart they had. In many Recent reptiles the heart, unlike that of mammals or birds, is a rather 'primitive' structure; the blood of snakes and lizards is never entirely cleansed of impure substances. This causes the animals to tire quickly and rest frequently.

If the dinosaur heart was more like that of a mammal or a bird, the animal would have been more agile for longer periods of time. This type of heart and the placing of the legs nearer to the body, would have made the early dinosaurs very superior animals.

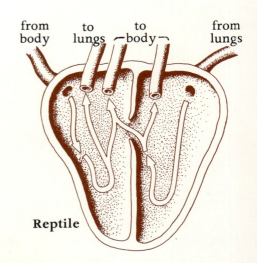

Above The reptile heart is not separated into four distinct chambers.

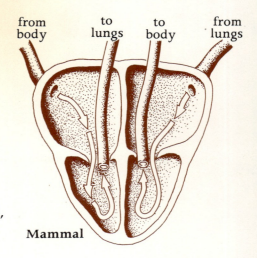

Above In mammals the heart has four clearly separated chambers.

Dinosaurs Rule the Earth

The Jurassic Period, 136–193 million years ago

The climate of the Jurassic Period was very different from that of the Triassic. It was wetter and as a result of the increased rainfall the plants were more varied and luxuriant. The landscape was reduced to low hills and the sea had invaded many lowland areas.

Below During Jurassic times the positions of the continents were different from today and the dinosaurs were spread out over many lands.

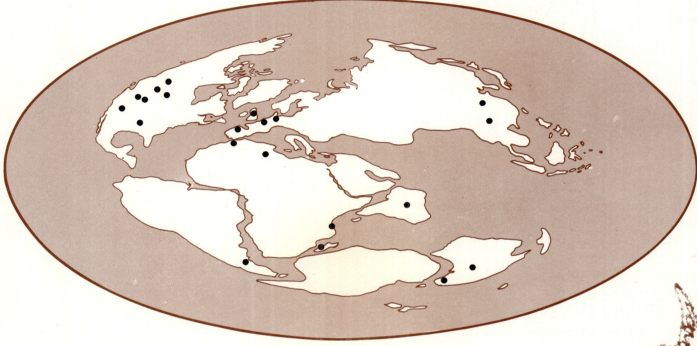

These seas were warm and shallow and filled with shell fish and vertebrates. They were ideal feeding grounds for the great marine reptiles, such as the plesiosaurs and ichthyosaurs. Nearer to land, marine crocodiles and turtles searched for food.

In the air the pterodactyls (ter–o–dact–isles) were supreme, their dominance to remain unchallenged until the end of the period and the evolution of the birds.

On land, lizards had appeared and although most of the mammal-like reptiles had vanished, the cat-sized tritylodonts (try–tile–o–donts) lived on. Their distant relatives, the shrew-like mammals, were more common but shy and nocturnal in habit.

Of the early dinosaurs, *Plateosaurus* and the first flesh-eaters had gone, their places occupied by new, more spectacular types. In a journey through the Jurassic Period we would encounter a host of different animals.

Scelidosaurus (Skel–eyed–o–saw–rus), the 'limb-lizard', roamed the world 185 million years ago. Around it the landscape is filled with fern-like plants. The heavily built plant-eater pushes the plants aside as it moves forward, its back is lined with rows of bony plates and the tail is capped by a row of vertical spines. How strange that an animal of this type and size, 4 metres in length, should have such a small head. *Scelidosaurus* is a 'bird-hipped' dinosaur.

Above *Scelidosaurus* was one of the first Jurassic dinosaurs.

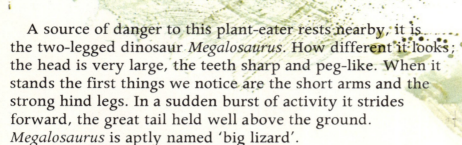

A source of danger to this plant-eater rests nearby, it is the two-legged dinosaur *Megalosaurus*. How different it looks; the head is very large, the teeth sharp and peg-like. When it stands the first things we notice are the short arms and the strong hind legs. In a sudden burst of activity it strides forward, the great tail held well above the ground. *Megalosaurus* is aptly named 'big lizard'.

As a carnivore, *Megalosaurus* illustrates that the 'lizard-hipped' dinosaurs have already separated into flesh- and plant-eaters, for in another land one of the earliest sauropod or 'reptile-footed' dinosaurs lives. It is named *Rhoetosaurus* (Wrote–o–saw–rus) and characteristically it has a long neck and huge body, and feeds on plants.

In a number of years these giant sauropods will spread throughout the world, their great bodies growing larger than those of any known land animals. The spread of these enormous beasts in many lands may have been helped by the greater number of swamps. The weight of the body may have forced the animals to spend most of their time in water, where, with much of their weight supported for them, they would be able to move about more easily.

In the Upper Jurassic (140 million years ago) the lands of our planet would have been dominated by the sheer size of these monsters. The remains of *Brachiosaurus* (Brak–ee–o–saw–rus) are found in the United States and east Africa, and these show that it was the greatest of all known land animals. It is possible to estimate the weight at between 40 and 70 tonnes. To see one in life would have been a fantastic experience. Imagine the scene.

The horizon is broken by hills and forests of cycads grow down to the edge of the swamps. A huge shadow crosses the sunlit soil, the water is disturbed and waves lap along the shoreline. The greatest beast of all time walks slowly towards some plants. *Brachiosaurus*, or the 'arm lizard' stands before us. Its head is over 12 metres above the ground, the tail disappears into the water, some 20 metres away. The head is ridiculously small, placed on the end of a long neck, whilst the body is very stout and supported on four strong legs. Unlike other forms, the front legs are longer than the hind ones, a character which may be of use when standing in the deeper waters of the swamp.

Another sauropod, *Diplodocus* (Dip–low–doe–kus), also lived amidst the swamps, of what is now the North American area, during the late Jurassic times. It belongs to a different family from the 'arm lizard', as its front legs are shorter than the hind ones.

Above Giant brachiosaurs wade in shallow water, a view with which some scientists would disagree.

Diplodocus is longer than any other dinosaur, including *Brachiosaurus*. The body is lower and slimmer and over 25 metres in length. The tail ends in a long whiplash, and apart from its great size it is the only defence the animal possesses against attack. *Diplodocus* may also use the whiplash to anchor itself when the water is running strongly. The great padded feet may help in this way too, for although they look like those of an elephant, they have powerful claws.

When feeding, the huge reptile would rake water weeds or other plants into its mouth. The teeth are small and unsuited to any task other than eating soft vegetation. The small head is again typical of the sauropods and could only contain a very small brain.

Perhaps at the time when they needed to move to new feeding grounds, because conditions around them were deteriorating, their intelligence was such that they 'forgot' what to do and gradually died out in an inhospitable area. From the evidence available it is known that no 'second brain' was present near the tail of the sauropods to help them 'think' and appreciate change. The misbelief that exists on this point is because the nerves to the legs were very big and where they met the swellings were much larger than the brain itself.

Apatosaurus (A–pat–toe–saw–rus), the 'deceptive lizard', lived at the same time as the other two giants. It was lighter than *Brachiosaurus*, shorter than *Diplodocus*, and its brain was smaller than theirs. When one emerged from its watery home to lay eggs, the great carnivores could look forward to a very large meal.

Brachiosaurus

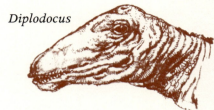
Diplodocus

Apatosaurus

Above These heads of giant sauropods show the shape of the skull and the position of facial muscles.

Below Many scientists believe that the large bipedal meat-eaters such as *Allosaurus* scavenged on carcasses that had been killed or had died weeks before.

For like the other sauropods, *Apatosaurus* was defenceless against the attack of a determined meat-eater once it had stepped on to land. Under attack the beast would try to move away, back to the safety of the swamp, the great tail lashing at its tormentor. But the cunning of a dinosaur like the vicious *Allosaurus* (Al–o–saw–rus), the 'strange lizard', would be too great and soon the two would be locked in terrible battle.

Allosaurus moves quickly on its hind legs and the great jaws seek out the neck of *Apatosaurus*. The tail of the plant-eater thrashes wildly, and on one occasion *Allosaurus* is struck across the legs. It reels away under the blow but soon gathers strength for a final attack.

Apatosaurus struggles to reach the swamp and safety, but this is not to be. Blood pours onto the sand at the water's edge and the great beast collapses. The carcass has been cut in many places during battle and blood covers the jaws and sharp claws of *Allosaurus*.

The large carcass of the great sauropod will probably feed many flesh-eaters, and *Allosaurus* itself will return several times to pick at the massive bones. When all the flesh has gone, the meat-eater will hunt again, and the plant-eaters will again live in fear.

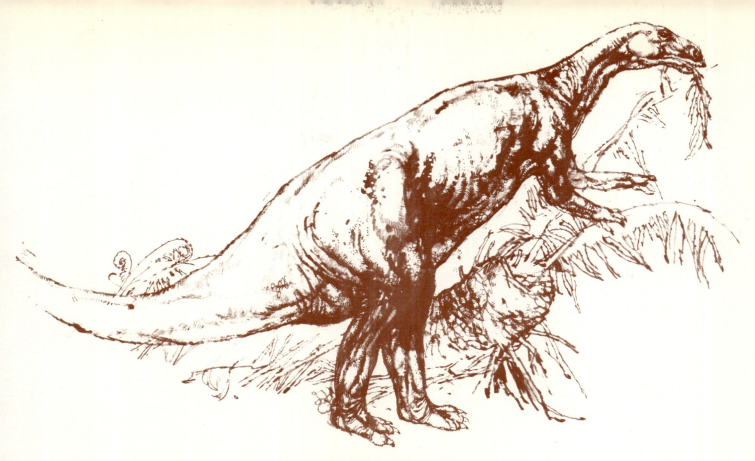

Camptosaurus (Camp–toe–saw–rus), the 'bent lizard', and its relatives feed in the same area as *Allosaurus*. But they are plant-eaters and only half the length of the carnivore. Different individuals range from 2 to 5 metres in length and the smaller ones could disappear in one swallow into the stomach of the 'strange lizard'.

It would be impossible to eat *Stegosaurus* (Steg–o–saw–rus), 'the roof-lizard', whole. For its back is lined with great vertical plates and the short tail is armoured with four long spikes. Unlike *Allosaurus* and *Camptosaurus*, it walks on all fours and the heavy armour is to protect it from the faster moving carnivore.

Stegosaurus lumbers slowly through the ferns, looking very much like its distant relatives of the Lower Jurassic. The head is very small and the jaws are beak-like. As with the other armoured dinosaurs, the 'roof-lizard' is 'bird-hipped' and the hind limbs are much longer than the front pair. In searching for some succulent fern fronds, it walks close to the swamps where the sauropods live. Several heads dot the surface of the water and in some cases only the high-placed nostrils indicate the positions of the great monsters.

The mud of the shoreline and the soil beneath the cycads is covered with small footprints. They must belong to dinosaurs less than a metre in length. The same prints could be found in many places at this time, including what is now North America and Europe. From their shape it is likely that they belong to small theropods or 'beast footed' dinosaurs. These creatures are lightly built, moving about quickly on long hind limbs. Their arms are small and slim, the clawed fingers being used for grasping small ground-dwelling creatures.

Comsognathus (Com–sog–nay–thus) is a theropod and is one of the smallest dinosaurs. The body is less than a metre in length and the skull only 5 cms long. One of the reasons

Above *Camptosaurus*, an ornithopod or two-legged 'bird-hipped' dinosaur.

Below *Stegosaurus* was 'bird-hipped' but walked on all four limbs.

why it runs so quickly is that it has slender, thin-walled bones. These are strong but light and reduce the weight of the body. Perhaps *Comsognathus* or its relatives chased and killed small mammals. They may even have eaten other reptiles or an early primitive bird. Speed would help a lot in hunting, particularly if the animal being chased could fly a little.

Such an animal was *Archaeopteryx* (Arc–kaye–op–ter–rix). It was the first bird and lived in the Upper Jurassic (145 million years ago). Unlike its descendants, however, it had teeth, and claws on the front limbs, which indicate a close relationship to the reptiles. Feathers covered the body and long tail, and these enabled the animal to glide through the air. It probably spent a lot of its life on the ground, and if attacked would run and launch itself into the air like a chicken. Sometimes it would climb trees and glide downwards with its wings outspread. As yet, however, true flight was unknown to these creatures and restricted to the flying lizards.

The pterodactyls or pterosaurs lived throughout the Jurassic Period and, as noted before, are related to both the crocodiles and the dinosaurs. They were not, however, the ancestors of the birds.

These reptiles varied in size across the wings from 12 cms to over 10 metres. Like bats, they were lightly built and rather ugly. The head was large and the jaws filled with sharp teeth. A great wing-like membrane stretched from the tip of an elongate fore-finger to the hind leg. The smaller forms probably flew by beating their wings, whilst the gigantic types used air currents, just like great gliders. All of the pterosaurs were meat-eaters, feeding on insects or fish, depending on their size.

At first, all the pterodactyls had long tails but in the Upper Jurassic short-tailed forms appeared. Then the skies were shared by beasts such as *Rhamphorhyncus* (Ram–for–rink–us) and *Pterodactylus* (Tero–dak–tile–us).

Of the two, *Pterodactylus* or 'wing finger' was common along the shorelines of the Jurassic Seas. It was a small animal, about the size of a blackbird, and it flew over the waves in search of fish. Now and again it would swoop down and snatch at a fish swimming near the surface. Perhaps it would then return to land and feed the young pterodactyls which had emerged from eggs laid on an earlier visit.

In the waters of the seas the competition for food and the fight for survival was dominated by the largest marine reptiles.

The fish-like ichthyosaurs lived all of their lives in warm waters, for although their streamlined bodies were ideal for swimming, they were useless for crawling up a beach to lay eggs. To overcome this problem, the ichthyosaurs hatched their eggs inside the body and gave birth to young replicas of themselves.

Ichthyosaurs look a little like dolphins or porpoises and could probably dive to the depths of Jurassic seas. Rows of sharp pointed teeth indicate that they fed on fish and other animals. The larger ichthyosaurs grew to 7 metres in length.

If we take a look at marine life in the Jurassic, we see that the heads of the ichthyosaurs are long, with large eyes.

Above In Southern Germany rocks of Jurassic age contain many fossils, including pterodactyls, *Comsognathus* and *Archaeopteryx*. It is possible that *Comsognathus* attacked *Archaeopteryx*.

The limbs are fin-like, the front ones being much larger than the hind pair. The high triangular fin on the back is like that of a shark.

The plesiosaurs swimming nearby are very different animals, although, like the ichthyosaurs, their ancestors were also land dwellers. Some forms had small heads and long necks, whilst others, the pliosaurs, had large heads and short necks. The pleisiosaurs grew up to 7 metres in length, whilst the largest pliosaurs reached 12 metres.

Cryptoclidus (Crypt–toe–cly–dus) is an example of the long-necked pleisiosaurs that abounded in Upper Jurassic times. It has a rounded body which is less adapted to life in the sea than that of the ichthyosaurs. The paddles are much larger and are used for swimming rather than steering. They are also very useful during the difficult journey up the beach to a safe nesting site.

Unlike the ichthyosaurs, these monsters could not give birth to live young and therefore it is probable that the females laid their eggs on land. What a fantastic sight it must have been to see these animals, perhaps in hundreds, clumsily lumbering up a secluded beach to lay their eggs.

When the young pleisiosaurs hatched they would probably face all the problems of survival of a young sea turtle. Meat-eaters and egg suckers would prey on the eggs and young hatchlings, whilst pterodactyls would swoop out of the sky and snatch up the unlucky infants as they rushed headlong for the water.

The tiny pleisiosaurs who reached the safety of the water probably swam many hundreds of miles to their feeding grounds. There they would feed and grow until old enough to breed and return to the beach where life for them began. Every generation this cycle would repeat itself; it lasted for many millions of years throughout the Jurassic and Cretaceous Periods.

During their very long presence on this planet, the pleisiosaurs and ichthyosaurs outlived a variety of marine animals. In the late Jurassic the sea-going turtles and crocodiles developed. The crocodiles that turned to the sea as a way of life were rather strange creatures. They were known as the geosaurs and can be recognised by skeletal features which helped them swim and feed. They were unarmoured and the limbs were paddle-like. In *Geosaurus* (Gee–o–saw–rus) we see that the hind limbs are much longer than the front ones, and the tail is broad and flat. In fact, it is very similar to the tail of an ichthyosaur and it enabled the sea crocodile to swim very, very quickly. Like *Cryptoclidus*, *Geosaurus* spent most of its life at sea, only going ashore to lay eggs.

The sea crocodiles became quite common in late Jurassic seas, but whereas the 'fish lizards' and pleisiosaurs survive to dominate the Cretaceous, the sea crocodiles were unsuccessful and soon disappeared.

The dinosaurs were successful and they survive the passing of the Jurassic Period. They cross the imaginary boundaries of geological time and even though the climate changed they continue to rule the world in Cretaceous times.

Above *Cryptoclidus* probably laid eggs on land rather than giving birth to live young in the sea.

Below The geosaurs had paddle-like limbs and fish-like tails.

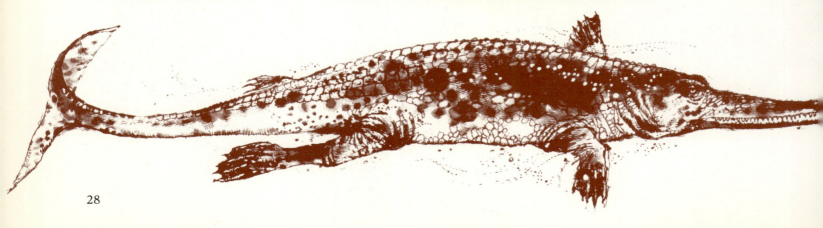

A Period of Change

The Cretaceous Period, 65–136 million years ago

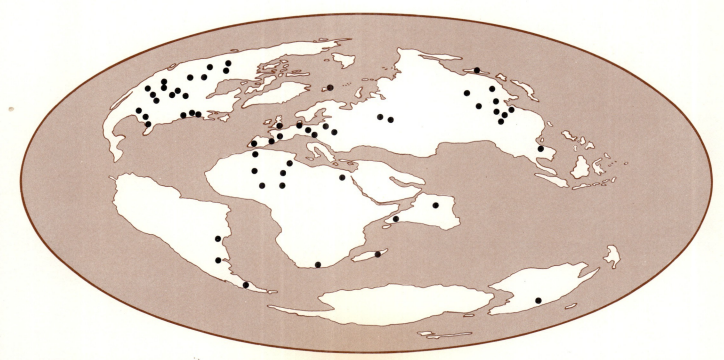

Below This reconstruction of the Cretaceous world shows the position of continents and the distribution of dinosaurs.

Below *Polacanthus*, an ankylosaur, was a four-legged ornithischian.

As with the Triassic and Jurassic Periods, it is possible to reconstruct the conditions that existed in the homelands of the Cretaceous dinosaurs. The task is a difficult one but, once again, we can use the sediments and fossil plants and animals in our reconstruction. The evidence buried in Cretaceous rocks tells us a story of fantastic importance to earth scientists.

The world was changing; the weather was milder, the temperatures cooler, perhaps the air was crisper. In some areas swamps still exist but they are less common than before. Ferns, horsetails and conifers are abundant, and many animals depend on these plants for their food. Elsewhere, however, the countryside is drier and rolls out before us with only small hills breaking the skyline. Remains of plants preserved in the rocks tell us that flowering plants such as the oak, poplar and plane grew in these areas. Their flowers brightened the countryside, their scents filled the air.

With the appearance of plants with flowers, insects similar to those of today flourish. They buzz busily to and fro, collecting pollen and helping the plants to spread far and wide.

Let us, with the aid of the illustrations in this chapter, return to the Cretaceous and take a close look at the animals that lived in those times.

The first area we visit is covered with ferns and small horsetails and the soil underfoot is soft and damp. From the green fronds of a clump of ferns our first Cretaceous dinosaur rumbles into view. It walks on all four limbs and when fully visible is seen to be armoured. Along its back are two rows of very large spines, the head is small, the body heavy. Scientists call this animal *Polacanthus* (Pole-a-can-thus); it is an ankylosaur or armoured dinosaur, a 'reptilian tank'. Amongst a group of these animals, the adults are about 3 metres in length. Together with the younger animals they wander slowly through the growths of ferns.

Because of the spines it is difficult to imagine any other dinosaur attacking *Polacanthus*. It would be very hard to hold and even harder to turn over to expose the soft belly. However, flesh-eaters do live in this area and, if hungry, they will attack even this well protected form.

In the swamp areas a few hundred metres from where *Polacanthus* is feeding, other herbivores can be seen. The giant sauropods are fewer than in the Jurassic Period; their places have been taken by other plant-eaters. Remember that, like today, different animals live in different areas, and the same is true of the dinosaurs. The map on page 29 shows the distribution of Cretaceous dinosaurs and the positions of the continents at that time.

Of the new plant-eaters, *Iguanodon* stands tall above the ferns and cycads. What a strange animal it is! The hind limbs are strong and massive, supporting the body in the upright

Above Iguanodonts probably roamed in herds with young and old together. They lived at the same time as the smaller *Hypsilophodon*, an active ornithopod, also shown here.

position. The arms are much smaller and quite slender, although in very old animals they are thought to have helped support the body weight. The hands are unusual, for the thumbs are spike-like and make evil looking 'weapons'.

An adult *Iguanodon* is over 5 metres in height and 9 metres in length. The body is very heavy and swollen in appearance, whilst the head is elongate and rather flat.

Small groups feed near the edge of the swampy waters, and the soft mud at the water's edge is marked by three-toed footprints. When one of the animals crosses the muddy shoreline, it swaggers from side to side and places one foot down directly in front of the other. If the mud is dried out and buried below new deposits, the footprints will be preserved for all time. (Trailways of *Iguanodon* have been found in Dorset, England, and elsewhere in the world.)

The ferns and cycads also give food and shelter to another bipedal plant-eater. *Hypsilophodon* (Hip–si–lo–for–don) is a 'bird foot' dinosaur like *Iguanodon*, but it is much smaller in size. The great spiked thumb is also missing. Amongst the individuals present the adults are 2 metres in length. When *Hypsilophodon* feeds it seems to cut plants between its jaws. In fact, the lower jaw has no teeth, a horny beak has taken their place.

Elsewhere loud noises disturb the plant-eaters; a dramatic event is taking place. A small animal is losing its life. In great pain it sinks slowly to the ground with blood spilling over its scaly skin. Deep wounds make a strange new pattern over its body.

Deinonychus (Dine–on–eye–cus) the terrible clawed dinosaur has caught and killed its next meal. It slashes at the body again and again, using its hind limbs. As another blow is struck, we can see that the foot has three toes, one of which is extra large and sickle-shaped. It is a powerful weapon for killing. Other carnivores gather to snatch a meal from the dead carcass. They approach quickly on two legs, their tails held high off the ground to serve as a balance during movement.

Some of the plant-eaters, frightened by *Deinonychus*, run away. They have long necks and very small heads; they look a little like ostriches although they have no feathers. In fact, their movements resemble those of birds, and *Ornithomimus* (Orn–ith–o–mimus) is aptly called the 'bird imitator'. The jaws are also bird-like. When feeding, the animal 'pecks' and grips the meat with its jaws and hands. Sometimes the strong hands are used to pull and tear food apart.

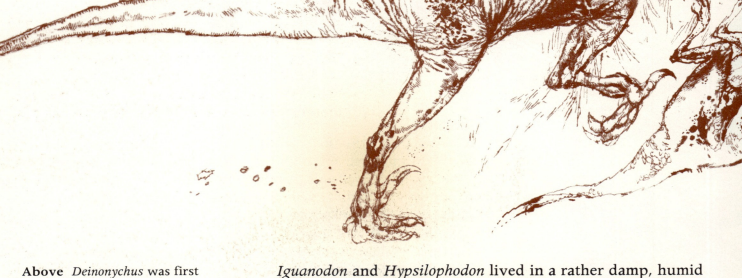

Above *Deinonychus* was first discovered in 1964.

Below *Psittacosaurus* of the early Cretaceous grew to about 2 metres.

Iguanodon and *Hypsilophodon* lived in a rather damp, humid climate in the area which is now the Isle of Wight. In a different land another type of animal existed which was probably a very important link in the story of dinosaur evolution. The climate of this land is not very different from that where *Iguanodon* lived, but *Psittacosaurus* (Sit–ta–co–saw–rus) is a very different type of dinosaur. It roams through the fern fronds, slicing the plant stems with its large parrot-like beak.

Psittacosaurus has a narrow face. Often the animal is seen to walk on all fours, but at other times it moves quickly on hind limbs only, and when it stops to feed the food is held in both hands. The size of the fore-limbs and the ability to move on either two or four legs indicates that *Psittacosaurus* is returning to walking on all four legs. Many scientists believe that it is, in fact, the ancestor of an important family of dinosaurs, the horned ceratopsians.

The progress towards the new family is slow, however, and *Psittacosaurus* lived nearly 30 million years before the first of the horned dinosaurs. During this long period of time other dinosaurs lived, died and became fossils.

Amongst these were the last of the great sauropods, such as *Titanosaurus* (Tie–tan–o–saw–rus) and *Mongolosaurus* (Mon–gol–o–saw–rus). These gigantic beasts continued the family line which we first met in the Jurassic. Then, however, their numbers were much greater and they lived in many more lands. In the Cretaceous, the number of species was smaller and the animals were found only in a limited number of areas.

The probable reason for the disappearance of these giants is the drying up of the swamplands, an event which took place earlier in the Northern Hemisphere than in the South, where the sauropods lingered on.

Other animals of the Lower and Middle Cretaceous (95–136 million years ago) included distant relatives of *Stegosaurus*, the large 'roofed' or 'plated' lizard. But these, too, were slowly but surely moving towards extinction, to be replaced in the Upper Cretaceous by a new armoured group, the ankylosaurs (an–ky–lo–saws). In fact, many of the 'ancient' groups were fading away and the new landscape was filled with interesting replacements.

The countryside of the Upper Cretaceous (65–95 million years ago) was really an extension of the drier areas of early times; swamps were of limited importance and flowering plants were everywhere. In some regions the weather was hotter, with little rainfall, the soil sandy and the vegetation brush-like. Boulders and pebbles were scattered over the surface of the open plain and they provided shelter for nests and eggs.

Below Discoveries by geologists in Mongolia prove that *Protoceratops* had a number of enemies, with one find showing two animals gripped together in death. *Oviraptor* is shown in the background.

The eggs were laid by the first of the horned dinosaurs, *Protoceratops* (Pro–toe–care–a–tops). Unlike his ancestor *Psittacosaurus*, this ceratopsian walks on all four limbs, but the front pair are still shorter than the hind limbs. The face is parrot-like, with a strong beak forming the upper jaw. At the back of the skull, a large bony frill is present, a feature shared with larger relatives. This frill of bone is for protection; the horned dinosaurs are plant-eaters.

Many families are represented in their early history by small animals, and in the case of the horned dinosaurs, *Protoceratops* is only a quarter of the size of the spectacular *Triceratops* (Try–care–a–tops). The largest *Protoceratops* is 2 metres in length.

The eggs laid by *Protoceratops* rest in a shallow nest, scraped into the sand. In time, they will hatch, the shell being broken open by the sharp beak of the young dinosaur. The youngsters emerge one by one and, exhausted from their efforts, rest in the warm sunshine. They are very small and unprotected; they would provide a good meal for a hungry predator.

At another nest the eggs will never hatch for *Oviraptor* (O–vee–rap–tor) the 'egg stealer' is feeding. This small dinosaur is a relative of the ostrich-like types mentioned earlier. In searching for food it darts quickly over the plain, and when a nest is discovered the 'egg stealer' breaks the contents with blows from its beak and hind legs. Having sucked the fluid from the broken eggs, *Oviraptor* moves on.

The young *Protoceratops* may have moved into a group of adults but some may be caught and killed. They are powerless to withstand an attack from the agile predator. They are held on the ground by the powerful hind limbs and killed by blows from the sharp beak. It is possible that when feeding *Oviraptor* was careless, for in one nest the body of one 'egg stealer' is seen amongst the cluster of eggs. It may have been killed by an adult *Protoceratops*.

Apart from *Oviraptor* other small, lightly built meat-eaters search for food amongst the exposed nests. These include *Velociraptor* (Vel–os–ee–rap–tor), the 'fast-running robber', and *Saurornithoides* (Saw–or–nith–oi–dees), the 'bird-like dinosaur'.

A large ankylosaur is also found in association with *Protoceratops*. Its name is *Pinacosaurus* (Pin–a–co–saw–rus) and, like other members of this tank-like group of animals, it is 'bird-hipped'. In comparison with our first horned dinosaur and the bird-like meat-eaters, the armoured ankylosaur is massive. Oddly it has a rather small head, a feature shared with other members of the two armoured dinosaur families. These well-protected plant-eaters are widespread throughout the world in the Upper Cretaceous. Small furry mammals also abound in the warm, dry lands where *Protoceratops* and *Pinacosaurus* lived.

On the American continent the armoured dinosaurs are very common. Groups of them wander across a landscape brightened by the growth of magnolia and laurel.

The bodies of *Nodosaurus* (No–doe–saw–rus) and *Scolosaurus* (Scoe–lo–saw–rus), the 'thorn lizard' are broad

Below The horned dinosaurs like *Monoclonius* roamed in herds, mixing with *Scolosaurus* (left) but aware of possible attack by *Gorgosaurus*.

and flattened. With *Scolosaurus* we can see many of the features of an armoured dinosaur. As it moves slowly forward in search of food, it is noticeable that the entire back is covered by a hardened platey skin. Rows of short, broad spines run almost from head to tail. The latter is short and fat, with two large spikes. The platey armour and spiked tail are excellent means of protection against possible attack. Like many other plant-eaters, the ankylosaurs reached great proportions; *Scolosaurus* and *Nodosaurus* both weighed approximately 2 tonnes and reached 5 metres in length.

Apart from the groups of armoured dinosaurs, herds of a new species of horned dinosaurs are appearing in the lands of North America and Asia. They are much larger than their distant relative *Protoceratops* and their horns and frills show a spectacular variety. Unlike the tank-like ankylosaurs, the ceratopsians probably relied on attack as the best line of defence. The cumbersome platey armour is missing and the body of the horned beasts is much more muscular. Perhaps like the rhinoceros, ceratopsians like *Monoclonius* (Mon–o–clon–ee–us) and *Triceratops* could charge at high speed and turn quickly enough to strike and possibly impale an attacker on their sharp horns.

To identify the different types of horned dinosaur, a palaeontologist would study the differences in the size and shape of horn and frills. Enough skeletons have been found to show that these dinosaurs evolved very rapidly in the Upper Cretaceous, and that eventually they represented twenty-five per cent of the whole dinosaur population of that time.

Some palaeontologists believe that vast herds of ceratopsians lived in America and Asia. They grazed on the bushy shrubs which covered the landscape. At times they would be attacked by meat-eaters which would probably pick on aged animals or youngsters separated from the herd. A meat-eater would have met many types of horned dinosaur in his search for food. *Monoclonius* had a single horn which grew upwards from just behind its nostrils. Two horn stubs were also present above the eyes. The whole head would be large enough to make even a ferocious meat-eater like *Gorgosaurus* (Gor–go–saw–rus) think twice before attacking.

Above Of all the horned dinosaurs *Styracosaurus* is the most spectacular.

The spectacular *Styracosaurus* (Sty–rack–o–saw–rus) would have been even more frightening to look at. Its horn was like that of *Monoclonius* but the frill was larger, with sharp spike-like outgrowths along the edge. The head is one of the most incredible characters of any dinosaur and must have given the animal a great deal of protection against attack.

Gorgosaurus and its close relative *Tyrannosaurus* (Tie–ran–no–saw–rus) must have caused havoc amongst the plant-eaters of the Late Cretaceous. These really were terrible lizards. They had great heads and a large number of vicious teeth. Like other two-legged forms, the arms were very small, while the hind legs were large and powerful. The jaws could open very wide and this suggests that these terrible 'twins' could kill and eat very large animals.

What a stupendous clash there would have been if an adult horned dinosaur was attacked by either *Gorgosaurus* or *Tyrannosaurus*. The ceratopsian would turn and twist, trying always to meet the meat-eater face to face. The attacker, on the other hand, would attempt to grip its prey behind the frill.

In a fight between *Tyrannosaurus* and *Triceratops*, the great carnivore would try to mount the back of the intended prey. The large jaws would open and close tightly on the neck of the plant-eater. *Triceratops* would resist violently and although smaller than its attacker, it was heavier and might break loose. In anger it would charge its attacker and inflict wounds with its great horns. Sometimes *Triceratops* would escape, having seriously wounded the most ferocious meat-eater of all time. Often, however, *Triceratops* would fail and die, its flesh torn apart by the sharp, curved teeth of *Tyrannosaurus*.

Right The enormous skull and rows of sharp teeth reveal the feeding habits of *Tyrannosaurus*. Here it battles with *Triceratops*. In the background is *Saurolophus*.

Other dinosaurs were not as well protected as *Triceratops* and had to move out of range when the 'tyrant' lizard was hungry. Some, like the duckbilled ornithischians, had no sharp teeth or powerful claws. Their skin lacked armour and they would have been easy victims if cornered. Many, however, had great crests. Their hands and feet were webbed suggesting that they were good swimmers.

They probably lived near water, pulling at leaves and twigs with the flattened beak-like mouth. The plant material was then crushed and ground by numerous rows of teeth. A noise would alert them; the great heads would be lifted high into the air. The approach of a predator would cause panic and the group would break up with many animals plunging into the water for safety. It is possible that the great crests increased the duckbills' sense of smell, which would warn them of approaching danger.

Saurolophus (Saw–ro–lo–fuss) lived in the same area as *Tyrannosaurus* and *Triceratops*. Like the 'tyrant', it walked on two legs when on land. The adults were smaller than the largest individual tyrannosaurs, being about 10 metres in length.

The great 'tyrant' and the three-horned *Triceratops* were amongst the last of the dinosaurs. The 'Age of Reptiles' was coming to a close. The giants of the reptile family became fewer and fewer in number towards the close of the Cretaceous. Never again do we see land animals of this size in the fossil record. Never again do forms like the great crested duckbills walk the lands of our planet.

The flight of a great pterodactyl, from high coastal cliffs to its feeding grounds in the Cretaceous seas, would link together the land of the dinosaurs and the dwelling places of the great marine reptiles.

Gliding high above the waves, the 'winged lizard' would have had a fine view of life below. But when it dipped down to sea-level it would have to keep a watchful eye for any potential attacker.

Below The savage hunter *Tylosaurus*

Above A long-necked pleisiosaur and *Kronosaurus*

Above The Cretaceous seas were filled with hordes of very different reptiles. Most were hunter-killers but the turtles ate plants and soft-bodied animals.

In the seas the marine reptiles which swam in search of food looked very similar to their Jurassic relatives. Some minor changes in the shape of the fins or tail had taken place to improve swimming and diving, but these were unimportant compared to the great changes amongst the dinosaurs.

The ichthyosaurs or 'fish reptiles' still hunt for food in schools, darting and diving through the waves. At first they are very common but gradually their numbers decrease and they were unimportant well before the end of the Cretaceous.

They were outlasted by pleisiosaurs and pliosaurs, which,

during the Cretaceous, grew to enormous sizes. *Kronosaurus*, a pliosaur found in the Lower Cretaceous, had a skull nearly 3 metres in length. In later times some pleisiosaurs measured 20 metres from snout to tail.

The giants ruled the waves for a long time but in the late Cretaceous they were challenged by a new group, the mosasaurs (mo–za–saws). They were true marine lizards, with large heads and a long slim body and tail. Rows of sharp teeth were set into pits and they rapidly disposed of the fish on which the animal fed.

Tylosaurus (Tie–lo–saw–rus) was an Upper Cretaceous mosasaur. It swam by beating its tail and moved left or right by movements of the paddle-like limbs. The great head and vicious teeth indicate that *Tylosaurus* was a very savage hunter.

Allopleuron (Al–lo–ploo–ron), a sea turtle, was no meat-eater, but like the mosasaurs lived the major part of its life in the oceans of the world. It had beak-like jaws and large paddles which pulled the light-weight body through the water.

The sea-turtles belong to several families but *Allopleuron* is a distant relative of the green turtle of the Atlantic and Pacific Oceans. Unlike the pleisiosaurs and mosasaurs, turtles survive to this day. The other great marine reptiles, like the dinosaurs, vanish for ever at the end of the Cretaceous.

Left Ichthyosaurs

Right *Allopleuron*

The Dinosaurs Vanish. We Ask Why?

Dinosaurs are absent from rocks deposited after the close of the Cretaceous Period, and this means that the last of these animals lived before the end of those times.

Birds, crocodiles and turtles lived alongside the dinosaurs and survived through to the present time. We can see them frequently in zoos or in the wild. If a group of modern animals died out, we would be able to list the reasons why. But no man has ever seen a live dinosaur and therefore the question of their disappearance is one of the great problems facing the earth scientist. The films and stories of men fighting dinosaurs and flying reptiles are intriguing but not true. The last dinosaur had vanished from the face of our planet millions of years before the birth of man (see chart on page 10).

The disappearance of the last of the terrible lizards took place over 65 million years ago and the problem facing us is like an enormous jig-saw puzzle. The pieces are numerous but, unlike our own jig-saws, can fit into several places. Over forty reasons have been put forward for the extinction of the dinosaurs but many of these are completely unscientific. In fact, it is doubtful if one reason alone could account for this prehistoric, wildlife drama.

Of the forty reasons, some are very bizarre and include far-fetched stories such as the visits to Earth of little green men from Mars in search of food. The list below gives some idea of the more silly suggestions.

1 Lack of standing room in Noah's Ark.
2 Movement of the moon from the area of the present Pacific Ocean.
3 Mass suicide, or dinosaur wars.
4 The blasting of the Earth's surface by meteorite showers.
5 Internal illnesses, including slipped discs and the reduction of the brain.

The cartoon illustrates the more humorous side of this story but the scientific point is also shown by the absence of dinosaurs in Tertiary times. Let us now consider the more realistic suggestions available to us.

We know that the Earth had changed during the Cretaceous, and that the flowering plants had become the most common type of vegetation. The climate had become milder and the continents had moved into the positions of the present day. Great forces also buckled and bent the Earth's surface into mountains and huge mountain chains appeared.

These facts are well known to the geologist and we can use them to support our ideas. Before the invention of cars and aeroplanes, travel between the different continents and over great mountains was very difficult; many lands and animals were unknown to man, they were isolated.

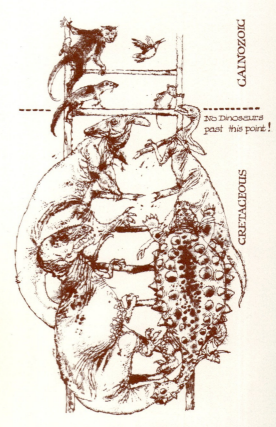

Above In our cartoon agile mammals mock the efforts of the dinosaurs to climb the evolutionary ladder.

At the end of the Cretaceous, the great new mountainous regions may have separated the dinosaur families. These mountainous chains, which include the Rocky Mountains, would have had the effect of draining the swamps where the water-dwelling dinosaurs lived. This, in turn, would have meant that the living conditions which had existed for millions of years would disappear. The competition for food and space would increase and probably reduce the number of plant-feeders. In turn, a reduction in the number of flesh-eaters would follow.

We know that mountain chains were formed but their effect on the dinosaurs is open to question. Apart from the change in the landscape, the effect of building mountains is to change the climate. This, in the Cretaceous, would be of importance to the dinosaurs, for if they were cold blooded a drop in daily temperature of a few degrees would reduce their ability to eat. Remember that reptiles are cold blooded and need the heat of the sun to become active. If a colder climate lasted too long they would have starved to death, for, unlike our own snakes and lizards, they were possibly unable to hibernate for long periods, and also they were much larger in size.

Any change in climate would also affect the plants of the time. New plants would develop which would be unsuited to the feeding habits of the plant-eaters. After a short period of time, those animals would die out and a break would appear in the food chain. In turn, the flesh-eaters would disappear and the dinosaurs become extinct.

Below The limbs of sauropods like *Brachiosaurus* are very similar to those of elephants, suggesting to a scientist a similar life-style and the ability to run very fast.

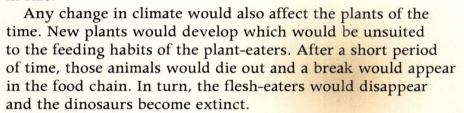

Below If the dinosaurs were warm-blooded then it is possible that *Chasmosaurus* ran like a rhinoceros.

This idea, however, although reasonable, has in recent years been questioned, as certain experts now believe that some dinosaurs were warm blooded. If this is so, then these dinosaurs could feed at all temperatures and the above suggestion would therefore not be convincing.

If the dinosaurs were warm blooded a drop in temperature would be less important. It would also suggest that these animals could move much faster than was originally thought possible. The conclusions from this idea would suggest, for example, that *Brachiosaurus*, whose head was over 12 metres above the ground and which weighed 70 tonnes, reached speeds of 25 kms an hour. These ideas are revolutionary and, as yet, are not completely accepted by palaeontologists. The idea that some dinosaurs were warm blooded is based, in part, on the structure of the bones, which seems to resemble that of warm blooded animals such as birds and mammals.

The illustrations on page 41 of *Brachiosaurus* and *Chasmosaurus* (Chas–mo–saw–rus) show that these animals, if warm blooded, would have moved in a very different way from that which had been thought of previously. They also show that more than one solution is possible when scientists try to explain the function of the animal skeleton. For example, we have seen that *Brachiosaurus* and other sauropods could be either swamp or plain dwelling animals, depending on the importance attached to various characters. This is like saying that a given animal could live either like the water-loving hippopotamus or an elephant, which prefers forested areas.

If one believes that these great animals were warm blooded, then a change of climate would be less important than a change in plant life.

Another reason which has been put forward, and one which has always been extremely popular, is that the mammals fed upon the unprotected eggs of the dinosaurs. Continuous plundering of the eggs would reduce the number of individuals in each hatching, and therefore have a direct effect on the number of surviving adults. If this number should drop below a critical level, the finding of a mate and the production of new generations would become very difficult. In the end this would lead to extinction.

Let us look at this reason critically.

The popular view is that agile, furry mammals broke and then ate the contents of dinosaur eggs. These eggs are thought to have lain relatively unprotected in shallow hollows covered by sediment or vegetable matter. If this is true, then amongst the numerous eggs found in the fossil record and attributed to dinosaurs, one would expect to discover that a large number of them would show obvious damage due to gnawing and crushing. This, however, is not known and it is unlikely because the mammals of the Late Cretaceous were very small, rat-sized creatures. Also, it is probable that by the Late Cretaceous, dinosaurs protected their nests in the same way as the alligators of the present time.

It is much more likely that the mammals, together with early birds, lizards and certain dinosaurs, attacked the newly hatched young. But as this had taken place throughout the history of reptiles, it is unlikely that it was the main cause in the disappearance of the group. It may, however, have been an additional burden to animals trying to cope with changes in the climate and plant life.

Near to the end of the Cretaceous Period, the continents had drifted further apart. The Atlantic Ocean now divided Africa and Europe from the Americas. Each land had a number of different climatic areas and the flowering plants differed considerably throughout those lands. Mainly, the plants resembled those of modern times, although the overall temperature was much warmer than today.

As a result of the movement and separation of the continents, the dinosaurs would have become isolated groupings. Disease or any other dramatic change which could affect the population would soon eliminate this once dominant group, for they would be unable to escape to more favourable lands.

Above Changes in the climate and plant life may have occurred during the Cretaceous and starvation and a lack of water may have caused groups such as the sauropods to become extinct. Here we see a dying sauropod.

Right Another popular view is that rat-like mammals plundered dinosaurs' eggs.

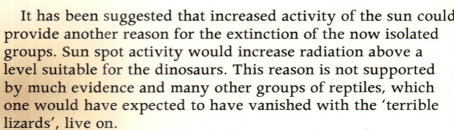

It has been suggested that increased activity of the sun could provide another reason for the extinction of the now isolated groups. Sun spot activity would increase radiation above a level suitable for the dinosaurs. This reason is not supported by much evidence and many other groups of reptiles, which one would have expected to have vanished with the 'terrible lizards', live on.

In conclusion, it is safer to say that a number of changes combined over a long period of time are much more likely to have caused the extinction of the dinosaurs. All other events are probably less important than the changes in the living conditions and the loss of suitable food.

No vast graveyards of dinosaur bones herald the end of the dinosaurs. Their extinction was a long, slow process of a group unable to change in time to meet new conditions. The small, insignificant mammals are about to become the most successful group of all time.

A recent suggestion by some palaeontologists, however, may throw some doubt on this belief, as they think that the birds are just feathered dinosaurs.

The Age of Mammals

Below Unlike the maps of earlier periods notice how similar this map of the Tertiary is to a map of the world as we know it today.

At the end of Cretaceous times great areas of dry land stretched across North America, whilst in Europe sea waters frequently flooded lowland areas. The climate was gradually changing to that of today, but early on in the Tertiary, parts of England were very much like Malaysia. Great tropical forests spread over the landscape and river banks were covered with luscious growths of palms.

Crocodiles and soft-shelled turtles thrived along the banks of the rivers, whilst on beaches great tracks mark the return to the sea of female turtles, who had just laid hundreds of thousands of eggs in the beach sands. Once in the sea, they were free from attack as the great marine reptiles had vanished. Only sharks which swam to and fro amidst the waves offered any danger.

On land many small mammals were being born but, unlike the turtle, they were born alive and protected and fed by their parents. Because of this, only small numbers were produced at birth and many of the dangers which would face a new hatchling turtle had been eliminated. In the absence of the dinosaurs and other great reptiles, the mammals spread rapidly throughout most of the world. Many new types of animal arose to occupy various positions in different lands.

In the early Tertiary the ancestors of the modern horse appeared in the forest glades of Europe and America. At first they were no larger than a small dog and their feet had toes, not hooves. These were the 'Dawn' horses or eohippids and they are found as fossils in Europe and North America. In time they were replaced by bigger animals which became more and more horse-like.

These changes in the evolution of the horse are seen in other groups of mammals and their histories are almost as

spectacular as that of the dinosaurs. Strange looking animals evolved to suit new conditions and cooler climates.

Between the death of the last of the great meat-eating dinosaurs and the appearance of the large carnivorous mammals, a group of enormous flightless birds arose to fill the vacant role. They grew to over 2 metres in height and their great heads, with powerful beaks, could easily kill any of the small mammals. Monsters such as *Diatryma* (Die–a–try–ma) must have caused havoc amongst the early warm-blooded animals. This giant would chase after its victim on its strong legs, outrun it and then kill it with a powerful blow from a clawed foot.

The gigantic size of these birds and their close relationship to the reptiles, seems to suggest that the relatives of the dinosaurs are having a final attempt at being supreme on land.

These birds would only be one spectacular example of life during the early Tertiary. A journey through the world at that time would have revealed a staggering number of different creatures. Some resembled hippopotamuses and others rhinos. Primitive rodents and carnivores were numerous and some forms show direct links with the pigs, cattle and camels.

Above *Diatryma*, a giant post-Cretaceous bird, killing a mammal.

Above Early horses like *Eohippus* fed on soft vegetation in forest glades. Their larger Recent cousins roam plains and eat wiry grasses.

Our story of the dinosaurs is complete, but a new one, revolving around the mammals we called shy and nocturnal, was beginning. It is sufficient here to look closely at the Eocene landscape overleaf to see how much things have changed and that a new order of life has come about. Apart from the 'Dawn' horses, larger plant-eating mammals, such as *Coryphodon* (Cor–rye–foe–don), abound. The reptiles are represented by small marsh turtles such as *Emys* (Ee–miss), and the crocodiles. In time the story on land will be seen in the oceans and rivers, for by the end of the Eocene the whales and sea cows show that the mammals, like the reptiles before them, had returned to a life in water.

To crown their victory the mammals also began to fly and conquered the air before the end of the Eocene. The flying mammals were the bats which in some respects look like the pterodactyls of times gone by.

In conclusion, it should be remembered that the success of the mammals was not the result of a vicious battle with the giant reptiles in which they emerged as the conquerors, but more the failure of the scaly-skinned animals to survive in changing environments. The mammals that have dominated the world since Eocene times include giants such as the extinct woolly mammoth, and the blue whale. But these are seen as gentle beasts when compared with monsters of the distant past such as *Tyrannosaurus* and its relatives.

Index

Page numbers in **bold** type refer to illustrations.

acid preparation 8
Africa 11
Age of Reptiles 16, 37
algal balls **11**, 11
Allopleuron **39**, 39
Allosaurus **24**, 24, 25
Altimira, Spain 9
America 5, 7, 13, 34, 36, 42
amphibians 11, 12
ankylosaur 29, 33, 34, 35
Apatosaurus **15**, **24**, 24
Archaeopteryx 26, **27**, 27
'arm lizard' 21
armoured dinosaur 29, 33, 34, 35
Asia 35, 36
Atlantic Ocean 12, 39, 42
Australia 11

bats 26
'beast footed' dinosaurs 25
Belgium 7
'bent lizard' 25
Bernissart, Belgium 8
'big lizard' 22
birds 26, 40, 43
'bird-hipped' dinosaurs 14, 15
'bird imitator' 32

Brachiosaurus **22**, 22, 23, **24**, 24, **41**, 41, 42
Buckland, W. **5**, 5

Cambrian Period 11
Camptosaurus **15**, **25**, 25
Carboniferous Period 11
Carnegie Museum, Pittsburgh, U.S.A. 7
ceratopsians 32, 35, 36
Chasmosaurus **40**, 42
chemical evolution 9
Coal Age 11
Coelophysis **18**, 18
Comsognathus 25, 27
Cope, E. D. **7**, 7
Corythosaurus 15
cotylosaurs 13, 14
crested dinosaurs 37, 38
Cretaceous Period 29–39
crocodiles 14, 16, 17, 18, 26, 40, 44
Cryptoclidus 27, **28**, 28
Crystal Palace **6**, 6
Custer, G. A. 7
cycads 18, 25, 31

'Dawn' horses **44**, 44
'deceptive lizard' 24
Deinonychus 31, **32**, 32
Devonian Period 11
Diatryma **45**, 45
Dinichthys **11**, 11
Dinosauria 6
Dinosaur National Monument, Utah, U.S.A. **7**, 7
dinosaur 'skin' 8
dinosaur wars 40
Diplodocus 23, **24**, 24
Dipterus **11**, 11

dolphins 14, 26
Douglass, E. 7
duckbilled dinosaurs 8, 36, 37

Earth, The 4, 5, 9, 15
Earth's Crust 9
East Africa 22
'egg stealer' 33, 34
'egg suckers' 28
elephants 23
Eohippus **44**
Eryops **12**, 12
Europe 7
evolution 9–13
 ladder of 19

Fabrosaurus 18
family of reptiles 13–15
'fast-running robber' 34
ferns 12, 18, 31
fish lizards 20
flying reptiles 20, 26
footprints 4, 16, 31

Geosaurus **28**, 28
Gorgosaurus **35**, 36

Hawkins, W. 6
heart
 reptile **20**, 20
 mammal **20**, 20
Heterodontosaurus **18**, 18, 19
horned dinosaurs 32, 33, 34, 35, 36
Hypsilophodon **31**, 31, 32

ichthyosaurs **16**, 16, 26, 27, 28, 38, 39
Ichthyostega **11**, 11